Wellspring
PRESS

ISBN: 978-1-956334-05-0

Important Information

Property Address	
Property Phone Number	
Property Management/ Owner Contact Information	
Internet/Cable Provider	
WIFI Network	
WIFI Password	
Hospital	
Urgent Care	
Grocery Store(s)	
Bait/Tackle, Fishing Supplies	

Our Local Favorites

Pizza	
Food Delivery Services	
Dine-In Restaurant(s)	
Activities	
Sightseeing	
Attractions	
Trails	

Miscellaneous Information

Miscellaneous Information

Our Message for You...

Dates of Stay	
Visitor Name(s)	
Visiting From	

We would love to hear about your stay. Please share your favorite places, memories, activities and experiences. We hope you had a wonderful time and come back to visit again soon!

May we share your testimonial? _____Yes _____No

Dates of Stay	
Visitor Name(s)	
Visiting From	

We would love to hear about your stay. Please share your favorite places, memories, activities and experiences. We hope you had a wonderful time and come back to visit again soon!

May we share your testimonial? _____Yes _____No

Dates of Stay	
Visitor Name(s)	
Visiting From	

We would love to hear about your stay. Please share your favorite places, memories, activities and experiences. We hope you had a wonderful time and come back to visit again soon!

May we share your testimonial? _____ Yes _____ No

Dates of Stay	
Visitor Name(s)	
Visiting From	

We would love to hear about your stay. Please share your favorite places, memories, activities and experiences. We hope you had a wonderful time and come back to visit again soon!

May we share your testimonial? _____Yes _____No

Dates of Stay	
Visitor Name(s)	
Visiting From	

We would love to hear about your stay. Please share your favorite places, memories, activities and experiences. We hope you had a wonderful time and come back to visit again soon!

May we share your testimonial? _____Yes _____No

Dates of Stay	
Visitor Name(s)	
Visiting From	

We would love to hear about your stay. Please share your favorite places, memories, activities and experiences. We hope you had a wonderful time and come back to visit again soon!

May we share your testimonial? _____Yes _____No

Dates of Stay	
Visitor Name(s)	
Visiting From	

We would love to hear about your stay. Please share your favorite places, memories, activities and experiences. We hope you had a wonderful time and come back to visit again soon!

May we share your testimonial? _____Yes _____No

Dates of Stay	
Visitor Name(s)	
Visiting From	

We would love to hear about your stay. Please share your favorite places, memories, activities and experiences. We hope you had a wonderful time and come back to visit again soon!

May we share your testimonial? _____Yes _____No

Dates of Stay	
Visitor Name(s)	
Visiting From	

We would love to hear about your stay. Please share your favorite places, memories, activities and experiences. We hope you had a wonderful time and come back to visit again soon!

May we share your testimonial? _____ Yes _____ No

Dates of Stay	
Visitor Name(s)	
Visiting From	

We would love to hear about your stay. Please share your favorite places, memories, activities and experiences. We hope you had a wonderful time and come back to visit again soon!

May we share your testimonial? _____ Yes _____ No

Dates of Stay	
Visitor Name(s)	
Visiting From	

We would love to hear about your stay. Please share your favorite places, memories, activities and experiences. We hope you had a wonderful time and come back to visit again soon!

May we share your testimonial? _____Yes _____No

Dates of Stay	
Visitor Name(s)	
Visiting From	

We would love to hear about your stay. Please share your favorite places, memories, activities and experiences. We hope you had a wonderful time and come back to visit again soon!

May we share your testimonial? _____Yes _____No

Dates of Stay	
Visitor Name(s)	
Visiting From	

We would love to hear about your stay. Please share your favorite places, memories, activities and experiences. We hope you had a wonderful time and come back to visit again soon!

May we share your testimonial? _____Yes _____No

Dates of Stay	
Visitor Name(s)	
Visiting From	

We would love to hear about your stay. Please share your favorite places, memories, activities and experiences. We hope you had a wonderful time and come back to visit again soon!

May we share your testimonial? _____ Yes _____ No

Dates of Stay	
Visitor Name(s)	
Visiting From	

We would love to hear about your stay. Please share your favorite places, memories, activities and experiences. We hope you had a wonderful time and come back to visit again soon!

May we share your testimonial? _____Yes _____No

Dates of Stay	
Visitor Name(s)	
Visiting From	

We would love to hear about your stay. Please share your favorite places, memories, activities and experiences. We hope you had a wonderful time and come back to visit again soon!

May we share your testimonial? _____Yes _____No

Dates of Stay	
Visitor Name(s)	
Visiting From	

We would love to hear about your stay. Please share your favorite places, memories, activities and experiences. We hope you had a wonderful time and come back to visit again soon!

May we share your testimonial? _____Yes _____No

Dates of Stay	
Visitor Name(s)	
Visiting From	

We would love to hear about your stay. Please share your favorite places, memories, activities and experiences. We hope you had a wonderful time and come back to visit again soon!

May we share your testimonial? _____ Yes _____ No

Dates of Stay	
Visitor Name(s)	
Visiting From	

We would love to hear about your stay. Please share your favorite places, memories, activities and experiences. We hope you had a wonderful time and come back to visit again soon!

May we share your testimonial? _____Yes _____No

Dates of Stay	
Visitor Name(s)	
Visiting From	

We would love to hear about your stay. Please share your favorite places, memories, activities and experiences. We hope you had a wonderful time and come back to visit again soon!

May we share your testimonial? _____ Yes _____ No

Dates of Stay	
Visitor Name(s)	
Visiting From	

We would love to hear about your stay. Please share your favorite places, memories, activities and experiences. We hope you had a wonderful time and come back to visit again soon!

May we share your testimonial? _____Yes _____No

Dates of Stay	
Visitor Name(s)	
Visiting From	

We would love to hear about your stay. Please share your favorite places, memories, activities and experiences. We hope you had a wonderful time and come back to visit again soon!

May we share your testimonial? _____Yes _____No

Dates of Stay	
Visitor Name(s)	
Visiting From	

We would love to hear about your stay. Please share your favorite places, memories, activities and experiences. We hope you had a wonderful time and come back to visit again soon!

May we share your testimonial? _____Yes _____No

Dates of Stay	
Visitor Name(s)	
Visiting From	

We would love to hear about your stay. Please share your favorite places, memories, activities and experiences. We hope you had a wonderful time and come back to visit again soon!

May we share your testimonial? _____ Yes _____ No

Dates of Stay	
Visitor Name(s)	
Visiting From	

We would love to hear about your stay. Please share your favorite places, memories, activities and experiences. We hope you had a wonderful time and come back to visit again soon!

May we share your testimonial? _____Yes _____No

Dates of Stay	
Visitor Name(s)	
Visiting From	

We would love to hear about your stay. Please share your favorite places, memories, activities and experiences. We hope you had a wonderful time and come back to visit again soon!

May we share your testimonial? _____Yes _____No

Dates of Stay	
Visitor Name(s)	
Visiting From	

We would love to hear about your stay. Please share your favorite places, memories, activities and experiences. We hope you had a wonderful time and come back to visit again soon!

May we share your testimonial? _____Yes _____No

Dates of Stay	
Visitor Name(s)	
Visiting From	

We would love to hear about your stay. Please share your favorite places, memories, activities and experiences. We hope you had a wonderful time and come back to visit again soon!

May we share your testimonial? _____Yes _____No

Dates of Stay	
Visitor Name(s)	
Visiting From	

We would love to hear about your stay. Please share your favorite places, memories, activities and experiences. We hope you had a wonderful time and come back to visit again soon!

May we share your testimonial? _____Yes _____No

Dates of Stay	
Visitor Name(s)	
Visiting From	

We would love to hear about your stay. Please share your favorite places, memories, activities and experiences. We hope you had a wonderful time and come back to visit again soon!

May we share your testimonial? _____Yes _____No

Dates of Stay	
Visitor Name(s)	
Visiting From	

We would love to hear about your stay. Please share your favorite places, memories, activities and experiences. We hope you had a wonderful time and come back to visit again soon!

May we share your testimonial? _____Yes _____No

Dates of Stay	
Visitor Name(s)	
Visiting From	

We would love to hear about your stay. Please share your favorite places, memories, activities and experiences. We hope you had a wonderful time and come back to visit again soon!

May we share your testimonial? _____ Yes _____ No

Dates of Stay	
Visitor Name(s)	
Visiting From	

We would love to hear about your stay. Please share your favorite places, memories, activities and experiences. We hope you had a wonderful time and come back to visit again soon!

May we share your testimonial? _____Yes _____No

Dates of Stay	
Visitor Name(s)	
Visiting From	

We would love to hear about your stay. Please share your favorite places, memories, activities and experiences. We hope you had a wonderful time and come back to visit again soon!

May we share your testimonial? _____Yes _____No

Dates of Stay	
Visitor Name(s)	
Visiting From	

We would love to hear about your stay. Please share your favorite places, memories, activities and experiences. We hope you had a wonderful time and come back to visit again soon!

May we share your testimonial? _____Yes _____No

Dates of Stay	
Visitor Name(s)	
Visiting From	

We would love to hear about your stay. Please share your favorite places, memories, activities and experiences. We hope you had a wonderful time and come back to visit again soon!

May we share your testimonial? _____Yes _____No

Dates of Stay	
Visitor Name(s)	
Visiting From	

We would love to hear about your stay. Please share your favorite places, memories, activities and experiences. We hope you had a wonderful time and come back to visit again soon!

May we share your testimonial? _____Yes _____No

Dates of Stay	
Visitor Name(s)	
Visiting From	

We would love to hear about your stay. Please share your favorite places, memories, activities and experiences. We hope you had a wonderful time and come back to visit again soon!

May we share your testimonial? _____Yes _____No

Dates of Stay	
Visitor Name(s)	
Visiting From	

We would love to hear about your stay. Please share your
favorite places, memories, activities and experiences. We hope
you had a wonderful time and come back to visit again soon!

May we share your testimonial? _____Yes _____No

Dates of Stay	
Visitor Name(s)	
Visiting From	

We would love to hear about your stay. Please share your favorite places, memories, activities and experiences. We hope you had a wonderful time and come back to visit again soon!

May we share your testimonial? _____Yes _____No

Dates of Stay	
Visitor Name(s)	
Visiting From	

We would love to hear about your stay. Please share your favorite places, memories, activities and experiences. We hope you had a wonderful time and come back to visit again soon!

May we share your testimonial? _____ Yes _____ No

Dates of Stay	
Visitor Name(s)	
Visiting From	

We would love to hear about your stay. Please share your favorite places, memories, activities and experiences. We hope you had a wonderful time and come back to visit again soon!

May we share your testimonial? _____ Yes _____ No

Dates of Stay	
Visitor Name(s)	
Visiting From	

We would love to hear about your stay. Please share your favorite places, memories, activities and experiences. We hope you had a wonderful time and come back to visit again soon!

May we share your testimonial? _____Yes _____No

Dates of Stay	
Visitor Name(s)	
Visiting From	

We would love to hear about your stay. Please share your favorite places, memories, activities and experiences. We hope you had a wonderful time and come back to visit again soon!

May we share your testimonial? _____Yes _____No

Dates of Stay	
Visitor Name(s)	
Visiting From	

We would love to hear about your stay. Please share your favorite places, memories, activities and experiences. We hope you had a wonderful time and come back to visit again soon!

May we share your testimonial? _____Yes _____No

Dates of Stay	
Visitor Name(s)	
Visiting From	

We would love to hear about your stay. Please share your favorite places, memories, activities and experiences. We hope you had a wonderful time and come back to visit again soon!

May we share your testimonial? _____Yes _____No

Dates of Stay	
Visitor Name(s)	
Visiting From	

We would love to hear about your stay. Please share your favorite places, memories, activities and experiences. We hope you had a wonderful time and come back to visit again soon!

May we share your testimonial? _____Yes _____No

Dates of Stay	
Visitor Name(s)	
Visiting From	

We would love to hear about your stay. Please share your favorite places, memories, activities and experiences. We hope you had a wonderful time and come back to visit again soon!

May we share your testimonial? _____Yes _____No

Dates of Stay	
Visitor Name(s)	
Visiting From	

We would love to hear about your stay. Please share your favorite places, memories, activities and experiences. We hope you had a wonderful time and come back to visit again soon!

May we share your testimonial? _____Yes _____No

Dates of Stay	
Visitor Name(s)	
Visiting From	

We would love to hear about your stay. Please share your favorite places, memories, activities and experiences. We hope you had a wonderful time and come back to visit again soon!

May we share your testimonial? _____ Yes _____ No

Dates of Stay	
Visitor Name(s)	
Visiting From	

We would love to hear about your stay. Please share your favorite places, memories, activities and experiences. We hope you had a wonderful time and come back to visit again soon!

May we share your testimonial? _____Yes _____No

Dates of Stay	
Visitor Name(s)	
Visiting From	

We would love to hear about your stay. Please share your favorite places, memories, activities and experiences. We hope you had a wonderful time and come back to visit again soon!

May we share your testimonial? _____Yes _____No

Dates of Stay	
Visitor Name(s)	
Visiting From	

We would love to hear about your stay. Please share your favorite places, memories, activities and experiences. We hope you had a wonderful time and come back to visit again soon!

May we share your testimonial? _____Yes _____No

Dates of Stay	
Visitor Name(s)	
Visiting From	

We would love to hear about your stay. Please share your favorite places, memories, activities and experiences. We hope you had a wonderful time and come back to visit again soon!

May we share your testimonial? _____Yes _____No

Dates of Stay	
Visitor Name(s)	
Visiting From	

We would love to hear about your stay. Please share your favorite places, memories, activities and experiences. We hope you had a wonderful time and come back to visit again soon!

May we share your testimonial? _____Yes _____No

Dates of Stay	
Visitor Name(s)	
Visiting From	

We would love to hear about your stay. Please share your favorite places, memories, activities and experiences. We hope you had a wonderful time and come back to visit again soon!

May we share your testimonial? _____Yes _____No

Dates of Stay	
Visitor Name(s)	
Visiting From	

We would love to hear about your stay. Please share your favorite places, memories, activities and experiences. We hope you had a wonderful time and come back to visit again soon!

May we share your testimonial? _____ Yes _____ No

Dates of Stay	
Visitor Name(s)	
Visiting From	

We would love to hear about your stay. Please share your favorite places, memories, activities and experiences. We hope you had a wonderful time and come back to visit again soon!

May we share your testimonial? _____Yes _____No

Dates of Stay	
Visitor Name(s)	
Visiting From	

We would love to hear about your stay. Please share your
favorite places, memories, activities and experiences. We hope
you had a wonderful time and come back to visit again soon!

May we share your testimonial? _____Yes _____No

Dates of Stay	
Visitor Name(s)	
Visiting From	

We would love to hear about your stay. Please share your favorite places, memories, activities and experiences. We hope you had a wonderful time and come back to visit again soon!

May we share your testimonial? _____Yes _____No

Dates of Stay	
Visitor Name(s)	
Visiting From	

We would love to hear about your stay. Please share your favorite places, memories, activities and experiences. We hope you had a wonderful time and come back to visit again soon!

May we share your testimonial? _____Yes _____No

Dates of Stay	
Visitor Name(s)	
Visiting From	

We would love to hear about your stay. Please share your favorite places, memories, activities and experiences. We hope you had a wonderful time and come back to visit again soon!

May we share your testimonial? _____Yes _____No

Dates of Stay	
Visitor Name(s)	
Visiting From	

We would love to hear about your stay. Please share your favorite places, memories, activities and experiences. We hope you had a wonderful time and come back to visit again soon!

May we share your testimonial? _____Yes _____No

Dates of Stay	
Visitor Name(s)	
Visiting From	

We would love to hear about your stay. Please share your favorite places, memories, activities and experiences. We hope you had a wonderful time and come back to visit again soon!

May we share your testimonial? _____ Yes _____ No

Dates of Stay	
Visitor Name(s)	
Visiting From	

We would love to hear about your stay. Please share your favorite places, memories, activities and experiences. We hope you had a wonderful time and come back to visit again soon!

May we share your testimonial? _____ Yes _____ No

Dates of Stay	
Visitor Name(s)	
Visiting From	

We would love to hear about your stay. Please share your favorite places, memories, activities and experiences. We hope you had a wonderful time and come back to visit again soon!

May we share your testimonial? _____Yes _____No

Dates of Stay	
Visitor Name(s)	
Visiting From	

We would love to hear about your stay. Please share your favorite places, memories, activities and experiences. We hope you had a wonderful time and come back to visit again soon!

May we share your testimonial? _____Yes _____No

Dates of Stay	
Visitor Name(s)	
Visiting From	

We would love to hear about your stay. Please share your favorite places, memories, activities and experiences. We hope you had a wonderful time and come back to visit again soon!

May we share your testimonial? _____ Yes _____ No

Dates of Stay	
Visitor Name(s)	
Visiting From	

We would love to hear about your stay. Please share your favorite places, memories, activities and experiences. We hope you had a wonderful time and come back to visit again soon!

May we share your testimonial? _____Yes _____No

Dates of Stay	
Visitor Name(s)	
Visiting From	

We would love to hear about your stay. Please share your favorite places, memories, activities and experiences. We hope you had a wonderful time and come back to visit again soon!

May we share your testimonial? _____ Yes _____ No

Dates of Stay	
Visitor Name(s)	
Visiting From	

We would love to hear about your stay. Please share your
favorite places, memories, activities and experiences. We hope
you had a wonderful time and come back to visit again soon!

May we share your testimonial? _____Yes _____No

Dates of Stay	
Visitor Name(s)	
Visiting From	

We would love to hear about your stay. Please share your favorite places, memories, activities and experiences. We hope you had a wonderful time and come back to visit again soon!

May we share your testimonial? _____Yes _____No

Dates of Stay	
Visitor Name(s)	
Visiting From	

We would love to hear about your stay. Please share your favorite places, memories, activities and experiences. We hope you had a wonderful time and come back to visit again soon!

May we share your testimonial? _____ Yes _____ No

Dates of Stay	
Visitor Name(s)	
Visiting From	

We would love to hear about your stay. Please share your favorite places, memories, activities and experiences. We hope you had a wonderful time and come back to visit again soon!

May we share your testimonial? _____Yes _____No

Dates of Stay	
Visitor Name(s)	
Visiting From	

We would love to hear about your stay. Please share your favorite places, memories, activities and experiences. We hope you had a wonderful time and come back to visit again soon!

May we share your testimonial? _____Yes _____No

Dates of Stay	
Visitor Name(s)	
Visiting From	

We would love to hear about your stay. Please share your favorite places, memories, activities and experiences. We hope you had a wonderful time and come back to visit again soon!

May we share your testimonial? _____Yes _____No

Dates of Stay	
Visitor Name(s)	
Visiting From	

We would love to hear about your stay. Please share your favorite places, memories, activities and experiences. We hope you had a wonderful time and come back to visit again soon!

May we share your testimonial? _____Yes _____No

Dates of Stay	
Visitor Name(s)	
Visiting From	

We would love to hear about your stay. Please share your favorite places, memories, activities and experiences. We hope you had a wonderful time and come back to visit again soon!

May we share your testimonial? _____ Yes _____ No

Dates of Stay	
Visitor Name(s)	
Visiting From	

We would love to hear about your stay. Please share your favorite places, memories, activities and experiences. We hope you had a wonderful time and come back to visit again soon!

May we share your testimonial? _____Yes _____No

Dates of Stay	
Visitor Name(s)	
Visiting From	

We would love to hear about your stay. Please share your favorite places, memories, activities and experiences. We hope you had a wonderful time and come back to visit again soon!

May we share your testimonial? _____Yes _____No

Dates of Stay	
Visitor Name(s)	
Visiting From	

We would love to hear about your stay. Please share your favorite places, memories, activities and experiences. We hope you had a wonderful time and come back to visit again soon!

May we share your testimonial? _____Yes _____No

Dates of Stay	
Visitor Name(s)	
Visiting From	

We would love to hear about your stay. Please share your favorite places, memories, activities and experiences. We hope you had a wonderful time and come back to visit again soon!

May we share your testimonial? _____Yes _____No

Dates of Stay	
Visitor Name(s)	
Visiting From	

We would love to hear about your stay. Please share your favorite places, memories, activities and experiences. We hope you had a wonderful time and come back to visit again soon!

May we share your testimonial? _____Yes _____No

Dates of Stay	
Visitor Name(s)	
Visiting From	

We would love to hear about your stay. Please share your favorite places, memories, activities and experiences. We hope you had a wonderful time and come back to visit again soon!

May we share your testimonial? _____ Yes _____ No

Dates of Stay	
Visitor Name(s)	
Visiting From	

We would love to hear about your stay. Please share your favorite places, memories, activities and experiences. We hope you had a wonderful time and come back to visit again soon!

May we share your testimonial? _____Yes _____No

Dates of Stay	
Visitor Name(s)	
Visiting From	

We would love to hear about your stay. Please share your favorite places, memories, activities and experiences. We hope you had a wonderful time and come back to visit again soon!

May we share your testimonial? _____Yes _____No

Dates of Stay	
Visitor Name(s)	
Visiting From	

We would love to hear about your stay. Please share your favorite places, memories, activities and experiences. We hope you had a wonderful time and come back to visit again soon!

May we share your testimonial? _____Yes _____No

Dates of Stay	
Visitor Name(s)	
Visiting From	

We would love to hear about your stay. Please share your favorite places, memories, activities and experiences. We hope you had a wonderful time and come back to visit again soon!

May we share your testimonial? _____Yes _____No

Dates of Stay	
Visitor Name(s)	
Visiting From	

We would love to hear about your stay. Please share your favorite places, memories, activities and experiences. We hope you had a wonderful time and come back to visit again soon!

May we share your testimonial? _____Yes _____No

Dates of Stay	
Visitor Name(s)	
Visiting From	

We would love to hear about your stay. Please share your favorite places, memories, activities and experiences. We hope you had a wonderful time and come back to visit again soon!

May we share your testimonial? _____ Yes _____ No

Dates of Stay	
Visitor Name(s)	
Visiting From	

We would love to hear about your stay. Please share your favorite places, memories, activities and experiences. We hope you had a wonderful time and come back to visit again soon!

May we share your testimonial? _____Yes _____No

Dates of Stay	
Visitor Name(s)	
Visiting From	

We would love to hear about your stay. Please share your favorite places, memories, activities and experiences. We hope you had a wonderful time and come back to visit again soon!

May we share your testimonial? _____ Yes _____ No

Dates of Stay	
Visitor Name(s)	
Visiting From	

We would love to hear about your stay. Please share your favorite places, memories, activities and experiences. We hope you had a wonderful time and come back to visit again soon!

May we share your testimonial? _____Yes _____No

Dates of Stay	
Visitor Name(s)	
Visiting From	

We would love to hear about your stay. Please share your favorite places, memories, activities and experiences. We hope you had a wonderful time and come back to visit again soon!

May we share your testimonial? _____Yes _____No

Dates of Stay	
Visitor Name(s)	
Visiting From	

We would love to hear about your stay. Please share your favorite places, memories, activities and experiences. We hope you had a wonderful time and come back to visit again soon!

May we share your testimonial? _____Yes _____No

Dates of Stay	
Visitor Name(s)	
Visiting From	

We would love to hear about your stay. Please share your favorite places, memories, activities and experiences. We hope you had a wonderful time and come back to visit again soon!

May we share your testimonial? _____ Yes _____ No

Dates of Stay	
Visitor Name(s)	
Visiting From	

We would love to hear about your stay. Please share your favorite places, memories, activities and experiences. We hope you had a wonderful time and come back to visit again soon!

May we share your testimonial? _____Yes _____No

Dates of Stay	
Visitor Name(s)	
Visiting From	

We would love to hear about your stay. Please share your favorite places, memories, activities and experiences. We hope you had a wonderful time and come back to visit again soon!

May we share your testimonial? _____Yes _____No

Dates of Stay	
Visitor Name(s)	
Visiting From	

We would love to hear about your stay. Please share your favorite places, memories, activities and experiences. We hope you had a wonderful time and come back to visit again soon!

May we share your testimonial? _____Yes _____No

Dates of Stay	
Visitor Name(s)	
Visiting From	

We would love to hear about your stay. Please share your favorite places, memories, activities and experiences. We hope you had a wonderful time and come back to visit again soon!

May we share your testimonial? _____Yes _____No

Dates of Stay	
Visitor Name(s)	
Visiting From	

We would love to hear about your stay. Please share your favorite places, memories, activities and experiences. We hope you had a wonderful time and come back to visit again soon!

May we share your testimonial? _____Yes _____No

Dates of Stay	
Visitor Name(s)	
Visiting From	

We would love to hear about your stay. Please share your favorite places, memories, activities and experiences. We hope you had a wonderful time and come back to visit again soon!

May we share your testimonial? _____Yes _____No

Dates of Stay	
Visitor Name(s)	
Visiting From	

We would love to hear about your stay. Please share your favorite places, memories, activities and experiences. We hope you had a wonderful time and come back to visit again soon!

May we share your testimonial? _____Yes _____No

Dates of Stay	
Visitor Name(s)	
Visiting From	

We would love to hear about your stay. Please share your favorite places, memories, activities and experiences. We hope you had a wonderful time and come back to visit again soon!

May we share your testimonial? _____ Yes _____ No

Dates of Stay	
Visitor Name(s)	
Visiting From	

We would love to hear about your stay. Please share your favorite places, memories, activities and experiences. We hope you had a wonderful time and come back to visit again soon!

May we share your testimonial? _____Yes _____No

Dates of Stay	
Visitor Name(s)	
Visiting From	

We would love to hear about your stay. Please share your favorite places, memories, activities and experiences. We hope you had a wonderful time and come back to visit again soon!

May we share your testimonial? _____Yes _____No

Dates of Stay	
Visitor Name(s)	
Visiting From	

We would love to hear about your stay. Please share your favorite places, memories, activities and experiences. We hope you had a wonderful time and come back to visit again soon!

May we share your testimonial? _____Yes _____No

Dates of Stay	
Visitor Name(s)	
Visiting From	

We would love to hear about your stay. Please share your favorite places, memories, activities and experiences. We hope you had a wonderful time and come back to visit again soon!

May we share your testimonial? _____Yes _____No

Dates of Stay	
Visitor Name(s)	
Visiting From	

We would love to hear about your stay. Please share your favorite places, memories, activities and experiences. We hope you had a wonderful time and come back to visit again soon!

May we share your testimonial? _____Yes _____No

Dates of Stay	
Visitor Name(s)	
Visiting From	

We would love to hear about your stay. Please share your favorite places, memories, activities and experiences. We hope you had a wonderful time and come back to visit again soon!

May we share your testimonial? _____Yes _____No

Dates of Stay	
Visitor Name(s)	
Visiting From	

We would love to hear about your stay. Please share your favorite places, memories, activities and experiences. We hope you had a wonderful time and come back to visit again soon!

May we share your testimonial? _____ Yes _____ No

Dates of Stay	
Visitor Name(s)	
Visiting From	

We would love to hear about your stay. Please share your favorite places, memories, activities and experiences. We hope you had a wonderful time and come back to visit again soon!

May we share your testimonial? _____Yes _____No